J. M. Armstrong

Voice of Melody

A choice collection of hymn tunes, for choirs, prayer-meetings, congregations, and

family use

J. M. Armstrong

Voice of Melody

A choice collection of hymn tunes, for choirs, prayer-meetings, congregations, and family use

ISBN/EAN: 9783337298227

Printed in Europe, USA, Canada, Australia, Japan

Cover: Foto ©Thomas Meinert / pixelio.de

More available books at **www.hansebooks.com**

THE VOICE OF MELODY:

A CHOICE COLLECTION

OF

Hymn Tunes,

FOR CHOIRS, PRAYER-MEETINGS, CONGREGATIONS, AND FAMILY USE.

BY

J. M. ARMSTRONG.

"For the Lord shall comfort Zion: he will comfort all her waste places; and he will make her wilderness like Eden, and her deserts like the garden of the Lord; joy and gladness shall be found therein, thanksgiving, and THE VOICE OF MELODY."—*Isaiah* li. 3.

PHILADELPHIA:
PUBLISHED BY LEE & WALKER.
J. B. LIPPINCOTT & CO.
1860.

PREFACE.

In adding, to the number of church-music books already published, a new claimant for popular favor, a few words of explanation may not be out of place.

Although many collections of sacred music have been recently issued, in but few instances has the convenience of the purchaser been consulted. Ordinarily, the volumes are too large to be conveniently carried from place to place, and generally contain much matter that is seldom of any practical use. Let the reader ask any one who is a member of a choir or is in the habit of using some particular collection, and he will find him familiar with perhaps one-tenth of the tunes in the book. A few new airs in each collection may command attention and secure popular regard, but the universal taste will be found to fix on the same old favorites. The remainder might almost as well be so much blank paper. The present work, it is believed, is not liable to this objection. With a few exceptions, the airs it contains are such as have proved themselves well adapted for use in devotional singing. The public must decide on the merits of the rest.

While not claiming much originality in performing his work, the editor must assume the merit of having, in many cases, restored the compositions to the state in which they came from the pens of their authors. Those who desire to hear every author speak for himself will, he believes, thank him for this. The same rule has been adopted with regard to the stanzas accompanying the airs. No practice is more reprehensible than that of altering the words of a sterling old hymn to suit the whim of an editor,—the author of a hymn alone having the right to alter it. In this work, therefore, the endeavor has been to give the stanzas in their original state,—it may be, however, with partial success.

A valuable feature of the book is its portability. During the Revival Season of 1858–59, many must have felt the need of a tune-book containing all the music requisite in prayer-meeting singing, and yet small in bulk. Such a want it is hoped this volume will supply. The fine quality of the paper, and the extraordinary beauty and legibility of the type, will certainly enhance its value as a pocket-companion.

The thanks of the editor are due to Dr. Lowell Mason, Mr. W. B. Bradbury, Mr. Horace Waters, and Firth, Pond & Co. for the privilege of using several copyrighted airs, and to others for original contributions. With this acknowledgment, the editor submits THE VOICE OF MELODY to the public.

J. M. A.

THE
VOICE OF MELODY.

Anvern. L. M.   Arr. Dr. L. Mason.

Triumph-ant Zi - on, Lift thy head From dust, and dark-ness, and the dead: Though humbled long, a-wake at length, And gird thee with thy Sa - viour's strength, And gird thee with thy Saviour's strength.

2 Put all thy beauteous garments on,
And let thy excellence be known;
Deck'd in the robes of righteousness,
The world thy glories shall confess.

2 So when the Christian pilgrim views
By faith his mansion in the skies,
The sight his fainting strength renews,
And wings his speed to reach the skies.

2 If aught should tempt my soul to stray
From heavenly virtue's narrow way,
To fly the good I would pursue,
Or do the sin I would not do;
Still He who felt temptation's power
Shall guard me in that dangerous hour.

3 Farewell, dear friends, I may not stay:
The home I seek is far away;
Where Christ is not, I cannot be:
This land is not the land for me.

4 My hope, my heart, is now on high:
There all my joys and treasures lie.
Where seraphs bow and bend the knee,
Oh, that's the land, the land for me!

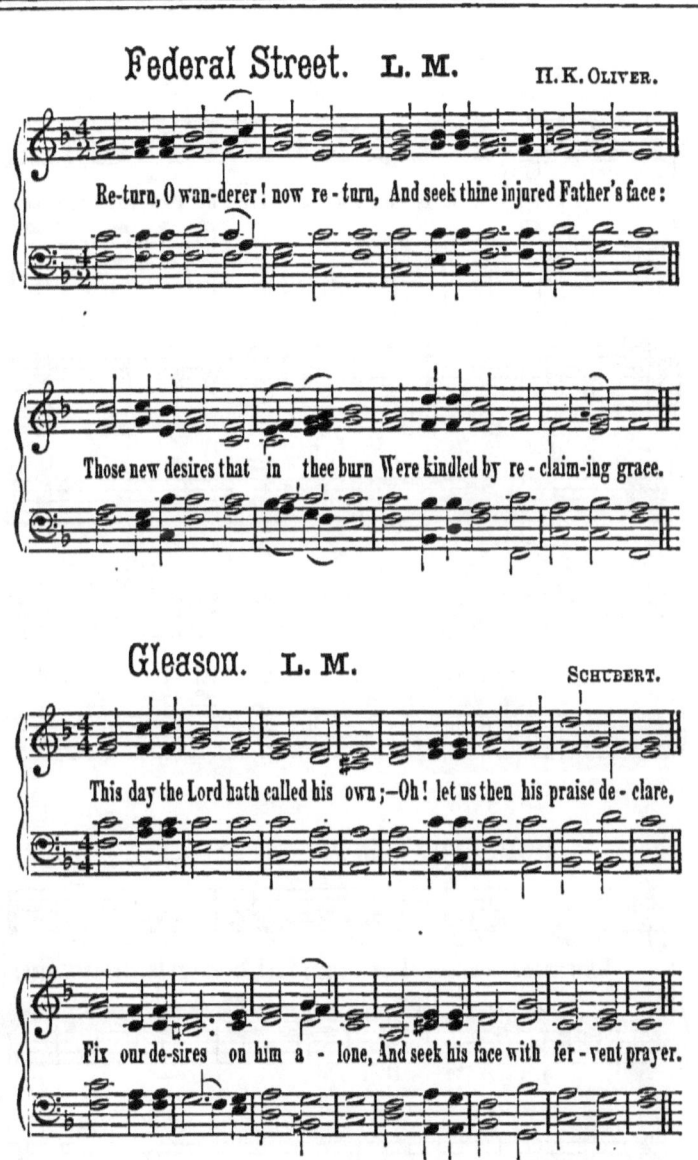

2 Lord! in thy love would we rejoice,
That bids the burdened soul be free;
And, with united heart and voice,
Devote these sacred hours to thee.

Louvan.

and sin-cere: When shall I wake and find me there?

2 Oh, glorious hour!—oh, blest abode!
I shall be near and like my God,
And flesh and sin no more control
The sacred pleasures of the soul.

Loving Kindness. L. M.

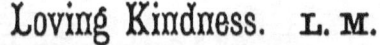

A-wake, my soul, in joy-ful lays, And sing thy great Redeemer's praise;

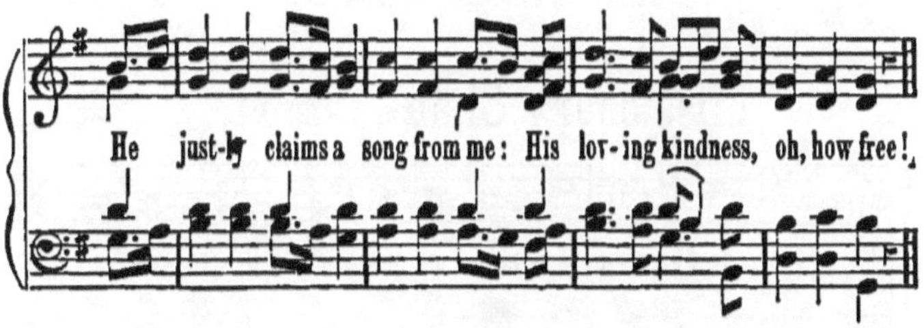

He just-ly claims a song from me: His lov-ing kindness, oh, how free!

Lov-ing kindness, Lov-ing kindness, His lov-ing kind-ness, oh, how free!

Mendon. L. M.

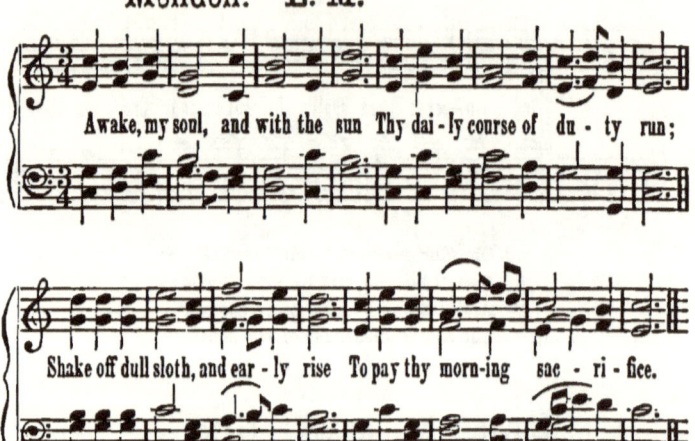

Awake, my soul, and with the sun Thy dai-ly course of du-ty run; Shake off dull sloth, and ear-ly rise To pay thy morn-ing sac-ri-fice.

2 Wake, and lift up thyself, my heart,
And with the angels bear thy part,
Who all night long unwearied sing,
"Glory to thee, eternal King."

3 Glory to thee, who safe hast kept,
And hast refresh'd me while I slept;
Grant, Lord, when I from death shall wake,
I may of endless life partake.

Missionary Chant. L. M.   Chas. Zeuner.

Ye Christian her-alds, go, pro-claim Sal-va-tion in Im-man-uel's name; To dis-tant climes the ti-dings bear,

Missionary Chant.

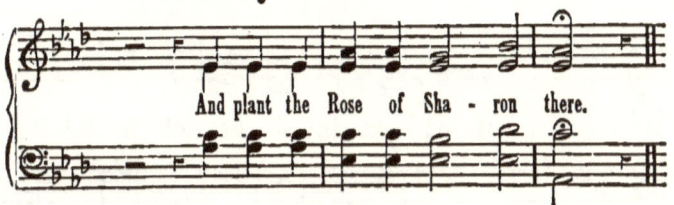

Migdol. L. M.
Dr. L. Mason.

2 Let thrones, and powers, and kingdoms, be
Obedient, mighty God, to thee;
And over land, and stream, and main,
Now wave the sceptre of thy reign.

Reliance. L. M.
I. B. Woodbury.

I lay my bo-dy down to rest; Peace is the pil-low of my head,
While well-ap-point-ed an-gels keep Their watchful stations round my bed.

Rest. L. M.
W. B. Bradbury.

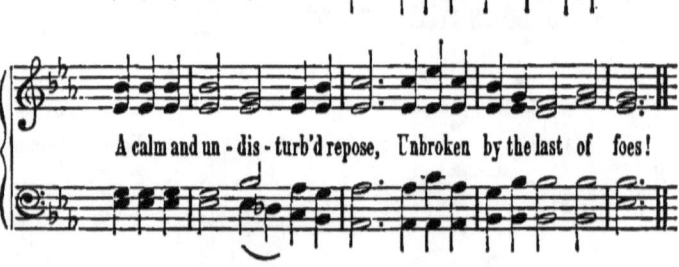

Asleep in Jesus! blessed sleep! From which none ever wakes to weep!
A calm and un-dis-turb'd repose, Unbroken by the last of foes!

2 Asleep in Jesus! oh, how sweet
To be for such a slumber meet!
With holy confidence to sing
That death hath lost its venom'd sting!

3 Asleep in Jesus! peaceful rest!
Whose waking is supremely blest;
No fear, no woe, shall dim that hour,
That manifests the Saviour's power.

2 "Give me a calm, a thankful heart,
From every murmur free;
The blessings of thy grace impart,
And make me live to thee."

2 Where is the blessedness I knew
   When first I saw the Lord?
   Where is the soul-refreshing view
   Of Jesus and his word?

2 Up to the hills, where Christ is gone
To plead for all his saints,
Presenting, at his Father's throne,
Our songs and our complaints.

Metropolis.

Meriden. C. M.

2 Sun, moon, and stars thy love declare
 In every golden ray;
 Love draws the curtains of the night,
 And love brings back the day.

2 O Lord, shouldst thou withhold them all,
    Yet would I not repine:
    Before they were by me possess'd,
    They were entirely thine.

3 Bright fields, beyond the swelling flood,
  Stand dress'd in living green;
So to the Jews fair Canaan stood,
  While Jordan roll'd between.

4 But timorous mortals start, and shrink
  To cross the narrow sea,
And linger, trembling, on the brink,
  And fear to launch away.

Aylesbury. S. M.
Dr. Green.

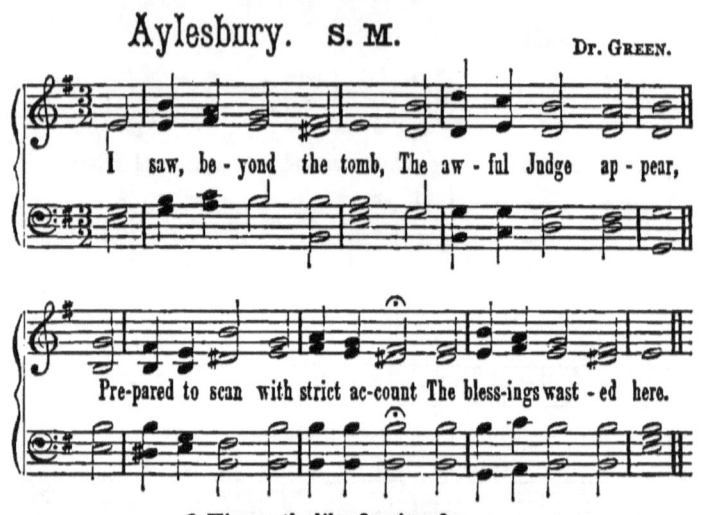

I saw, be-yond the tomb, The aw-ful Judge ap-pear,

Pre-pared to scan with strict ac-count The bless-ings wast-ed here.

2 His wrath, like flaming fire,
  In hell forever burns;
  And from that hopeless world of woe
  No fugitive returns.

3 Ye sinners, fear the Lord
  While yet 'tis call'd to-day:
  Soon will the awful voice of death
  Command your souls away.

Barre, or Meade. S. M.
C. Hommann.

Be-hold the morn-ing sun Be-gins his glo-rious way;

His beams through all the na-tions run, And life and light con-vey.

Bertrand. S. M.
G. Paesiello.
Arr. by V. C. Taylor.

Oh, bless the Lord, my soul, His grace to thee pro-claim,
And all that is with-in me join To bless his ho-ly name.

2 Oh, bless the Lord, my soul!
  Nor let his mercies lie
  Forgotten in unthankfulness
  And without praises die.

3 'Tis he forgives thy sins,
  'Tis he relieves thy pain,
  'Tis he who heals thy sicknesses
  And makes thee young again.

Beverly. S. M.
H. G. Nägeli.

Let songs of end-less praise From ev'-ry na-tion rise;
Let all the lands their tri-bute raise To God, who rules the skies.

2 Not as the conqueror comes,
    They, the true-hearted, came:
Not with the roll of the stirring drums,
    And the trumpet that sings of fame;
Not as the flying come,
    In silence and in fear;—
They shook the depths of the desert gloom
    With their hymns of lofty cheer.

3 Amidst the storm they sang,
    And the stars heard, and the sea!
And the sounding aisles of the dim woods rang
    To the anthem of the free.
The ocean eagle soar'd
    From his nest by the white waves' foam,
And the rocking pines of the forest roar'd,—
    This was their welcome home!

4 What sought they thus afar?
    Bright jewels of the mine?
The wealth of seas, the spoils of war?—
    They sought a faith's pure shrine!
Ay, call it holy ground,
    The soil where first they trod!
They have left unstain'd what there they found,—
    Freedom to worship God.

2 But, where the gospel comes,
It spreads diviner light;
It calls dead sinners from their tombs
And gives the blind their sight.

2 Here in the body pent,
Absent from him I roam,
Yet nightly pitch my moving tent
A day's march nearer home.

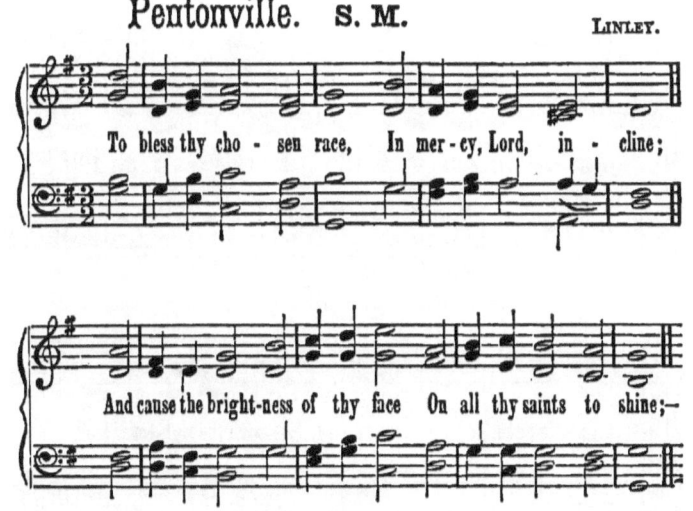

2 That so thy wondrous way
  May through the world be known;
  While distant lands their homage pay,
  And thy salvation own.

2 In every state secure,
   Kept by Jehovah's eye;
'Tis well with them while life endures,
   And well when call'd to die.

2 My gracious God! how plain
Are thy directions given!
Oh, may I never read in vain,
But find the path to heaven.

Silver Street. S. M.

I. Smith.

Come, sound his praise a-broad, And hymns of glo-ry sing;
T. S.
Je-ho-vah is the sov'-reign God, The u-ni-ver-sal King.

Southwell. S. M.

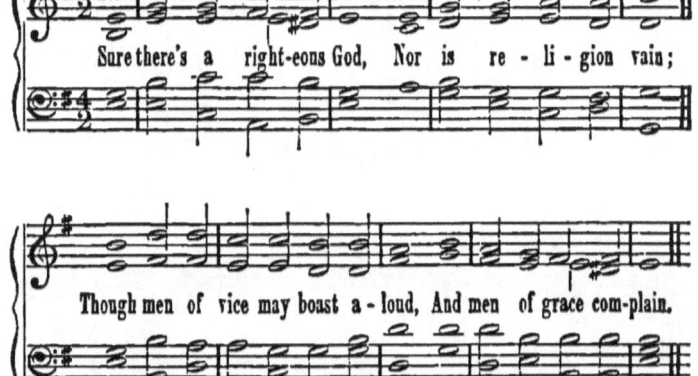

Sure there's a right-eous God, Nor is re-li-gion vain;
Though men of vice may boast a-loud, And men of grace com-plain.

2 I saw the wicked rise,
   And felt my heart repine,
While haughty fools, with scornful eyes,
   In robes of honor shine.

State Street. S. M.
J. C. WOODMAN.

Welcome, sweet day of rest, That saw the Lord arise;
Welcome to this reviving breast And these rejoicing eyes!

2 The King himself comes near,
And feasts his saints to-day;
Here we may sit, and see him here,
And love, and praise, and pray.

St. Thomas. S. M.
HANDEL.

Jesus, who knows full well The heart of ev'ry saint,
Invites us all our griefs to tell, To pray and never faint.

2 How will my heart endure
　　The terrors of that day,
　When earth and heaven before his face
　　Astonish'd shrink away?

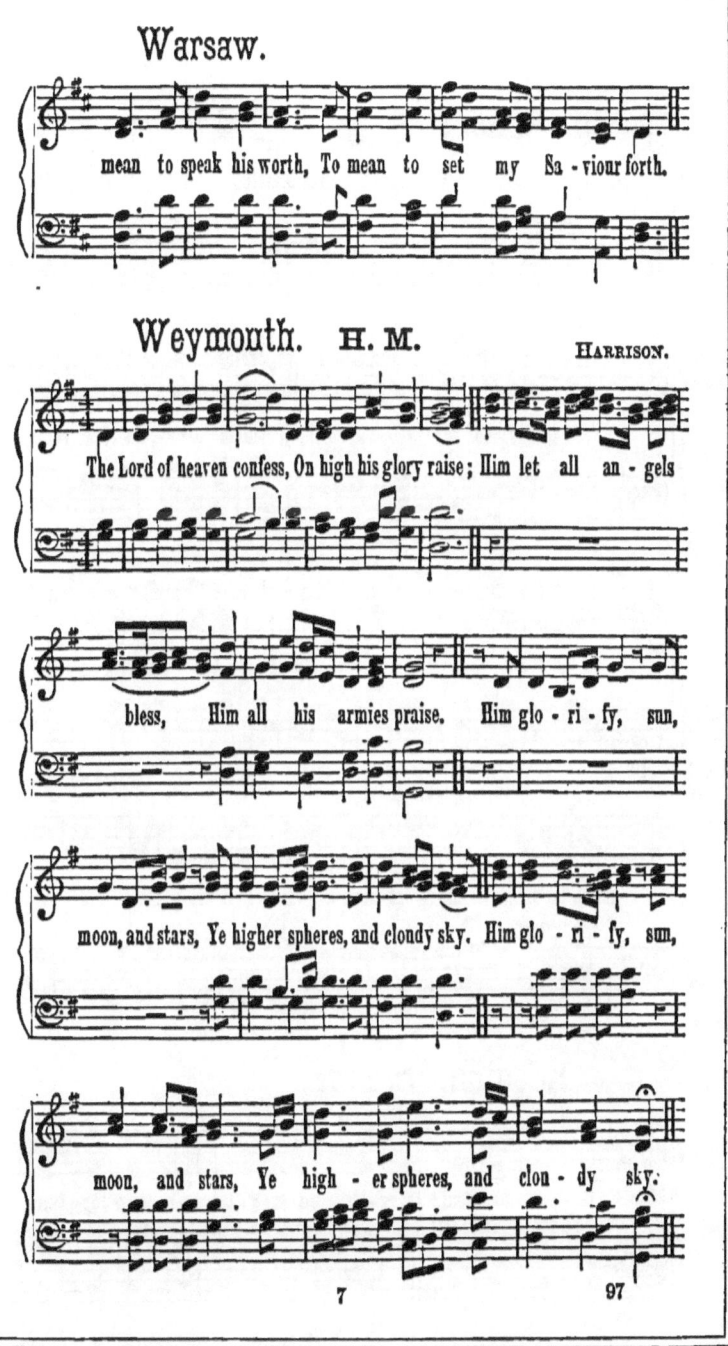

2 I heard the law its thunders roll,
While guilt lay heavy on my soul,—
A vast, oppressive load:
All creature-aid I saw was vain:
The sinner " must be born again,"
Or drink the wrath of God.

2 Upheld by thy commands,
The world securely stands,
And skies and stars obey thy word;
Thy throne was fix'd on high
Before the starry sky:
Eternal is thy kingdom, Lord.

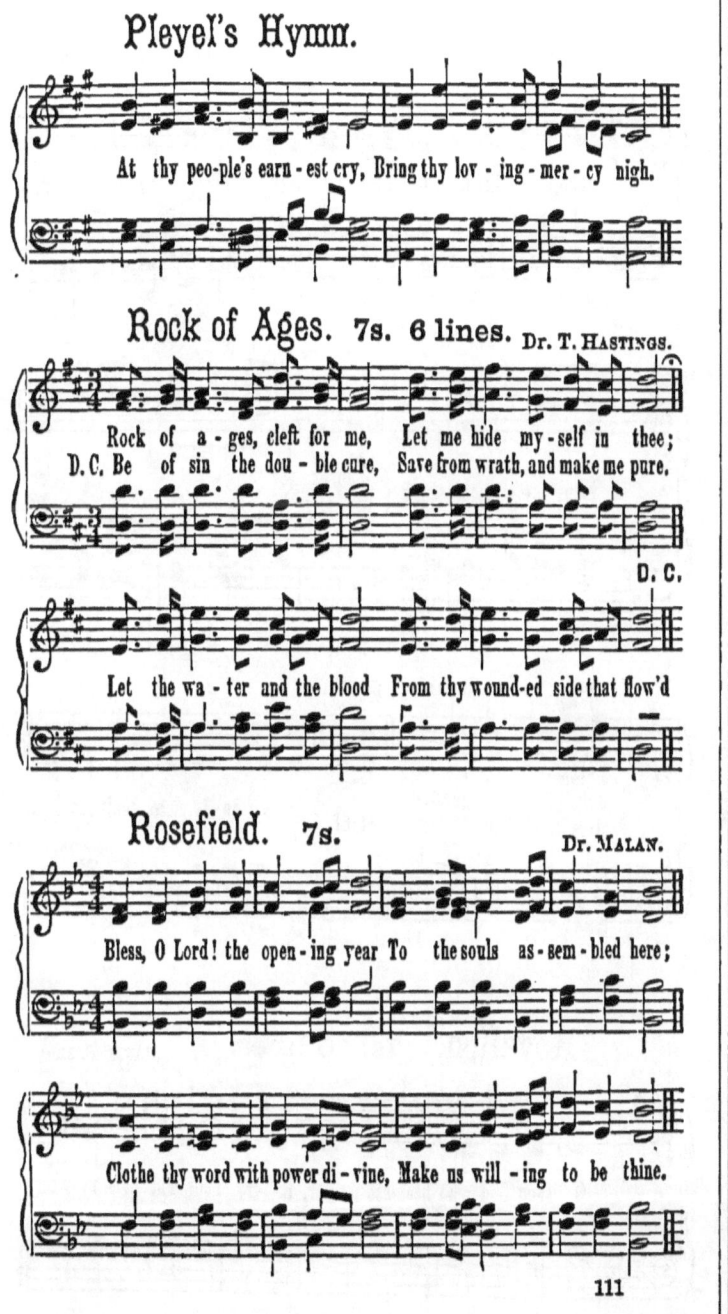

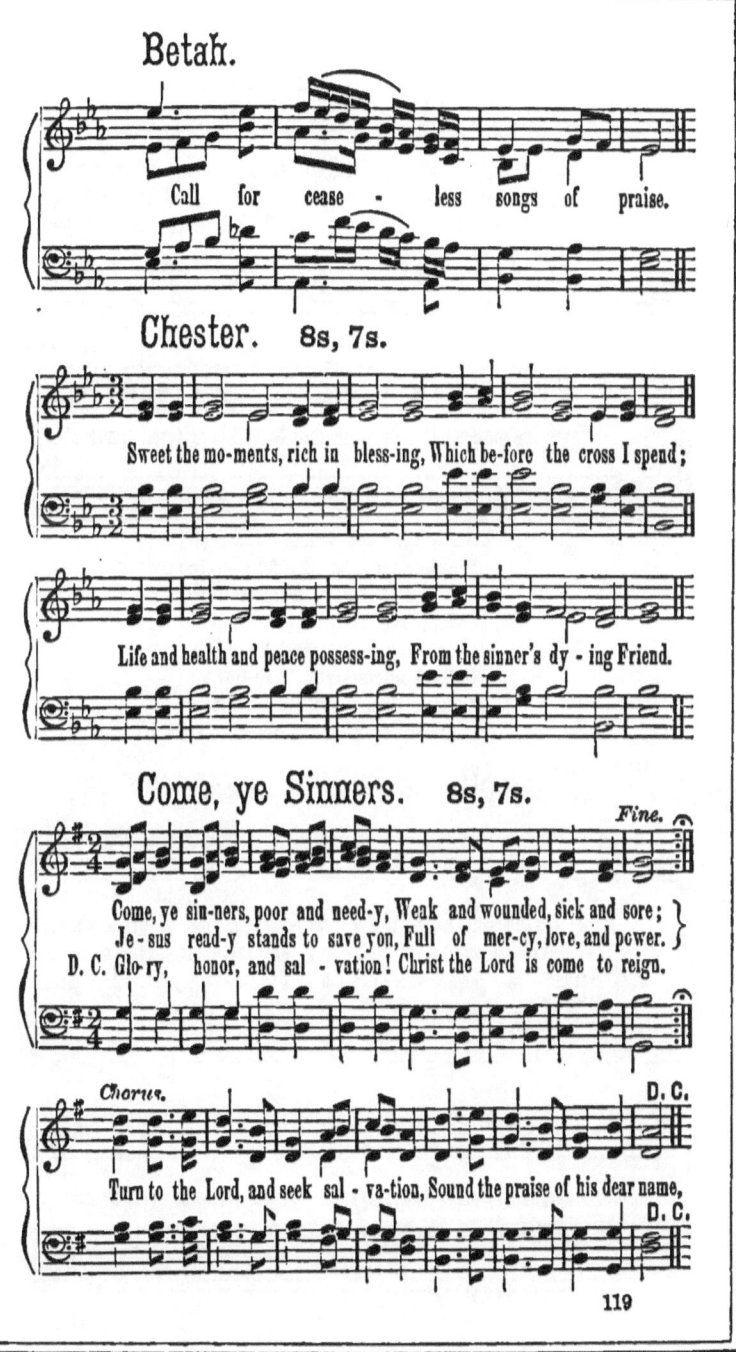

Greenville. 8s, 7s.

J. J. ROUSSEAU.

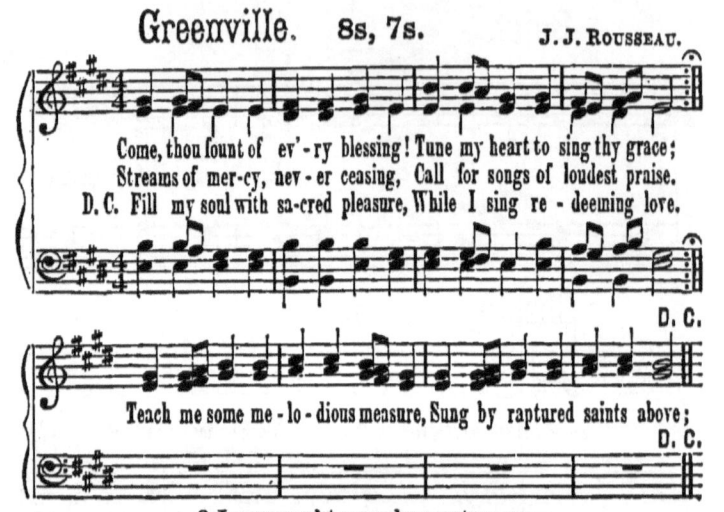

Come, thou fount of ev'-ry blessing! Tune my heart to sing thy grace;
Streams of mer-cy, nev-er ceasing, Call for songs of loudest praise.
D. C. Fill my soul with sa-cred pleasure, While I sing re-deeming love.

Teach me some me-lo-dious measure, Sung by raptured saints above;
D. C.

2 Jesus sought me when a stranger,
Wandering from the fold of God;
He, to save my soul from danger,
Interposed his precious blood.
Oh! to grace how great a debtor
Daily I'm constrain'd to be!
Let thy grace, Lord, like a fetter
Bind my wandering heart to thee.

Harwell. 8s, 7s. 8 lines.

Hark! ten thousand harps and voi-ces Sound the note of praise above;
Je-sus reigns, and heaven rejoi-ces; Je-sus reigns, the God of love:
D. C. Hal-le-lu-jah! Hal-le-lu-jah! Hal-le-lu-jah! A-men.

See, he sits on yonder throne, Je-sus rules the world a-lone.
D. C.

2 Praise, my soul, the God that sought thee,
    Wretched wanderer, far astray,
Found thee lost, and kindly brought thee
    From the paths of death away;
Praise, with love's devoutest feeling,
    Him who saw thy guilt-born fear
And, the light of hope revealing,
    Bade the blood-stain'd cross appear.

2 Listen to the wondrous story
   Which they chant in hymns of joy:—
   "Glory in the highest, glory—
   Glory be to God on high!"

2 Not to ease and aimless quiet
   Doth the inward answer tend;
But to works of love and duty,
   As our being's end.
Earnest toil, and strong endeavor
   Of a spirit which within
Wrestles with familiar evil
   And besetting sin.

Lyons.

Je-sus ex-tol; His kingdom is glorious, and rules o-ver all.

2 God ruleth on high, almighty to save;
And still he is nigh; his presence we have;
The great congregation his triumph shall sing,
Ascribing salvation to Jesus our King.

Peoria, or Eden. 12s, 11s.

{ How sweet to re-flect on the joys that a-wait me In yon bliss-ful
{ Where glo-ri-fied spi-rits with welcome shall greet me And lead me to

region, the ha-ven of rest, ⎫ En-cir-cled with light, and with glory en-
mansions prepared for the blest! ⎭ I'll bathe in the o-cean of plea-sure un-

1st time.   2d time.

shrouded, My hap-pi-ness perfect, my mind's sky unclouded,
bounded, And range with delight thro' the [OMIT........] E-den of Love.

2 Ye saints, who stand nearer than they,
And cast your bright crowns at his feet,
His grace and his glory display,
And all his rich mercy repeat:
He snatch'd you from hell and the grave,
He ransom'd from death and despair,
For you he was mighty to save,
Almighty to bring you safe there.

Homeward Bound.*

ARR. by J. W. DADMUN.

{ Out on an o-cean all-bound-less we ride, We're homeward
{ Toss'd on the waves of a rough, rest-less tide, We're, etc.
D. C. Pro-mise of which on us each he bestow'd, We're, etc.

bound, homeward bound. Far from the safe, qui-et har-bor we're

rode, Seek-ing our Fa-ther's ce-les-tial a-bode,

2 Wildly the storm sweeps us on as it roars,
  We're homeward bound;
  Look! yonder lie the bright heavenly shores,
  We're homeward bound;
  Steady, O pilot! stand firm at the wheel,
  Steady! we soon shall outweather the gale,
  Oh, how we fly 'neath the loud-creaking sail!
  We're homeward bound.

3 We'll tell the world, as we journey along,
  We're homeward bound;
  Try to persuade them to enter our throng,
  We're homeward bound;
  Come, trembling sinner, forlorn and oppress'd,
  Join in our number, oh, come, and be blest;
  Journey with us to the mansions of rest,
  We're homeward bound.

4 Into the harbor of heaven now we glide,
  We're home at last;
  Softly we drift on its bright silver tide,
  We're home at last;
  Glory to God! all our dangers are o'er;
  We stand secure on the glorified shore,
  Glory to God! we will shout evermore,
  We're home at last.

* From the "Sabbath-School Bell," by permission of H. Waters.

Land of Promise.

I have a Fa-ther in the promised land, I have a Fa-ther in the promised land; My Father calls me, I must go To meet him in the promised land.

Chorus.
I'll a-way, I'll a-way to the promised land, I'll a-way, I'll a-way to the promised land; My Father calls me, I must go To meet him in the promised land.

2 I have a Saviour in the promised land;
   My Saviour calls me, I must go
   To meet him in the promised land.
    I'll away, I'll away to the promised land;
   My Saviour calls me, I must go
   To meet him in the promised land.

3 I hope to meet you in the promised land;
   At Jesus' feet, a joyous band,
   We'll praise him in the promised land.
    We'll away to the promised land;
   At Jesus' feet, a joyous band,
   We'll praise him in the promised land.

2 No night shall be in heaven! no dreadful hour
Of mental darkness, or the tempter's power;
Across those skies no envious cloud shall roll,
To dim the sunlight of the raptured soul.
    No night shall be in heaven.

3 No night shall be in heaven. Forbid to sleep,
These eyes no more their mournful vigils keep;
Their fountains dried, their tears all wiped away,
They gaze undazzled on eternal day.
    No night shall be in heaven.

4 No night shall be in heaven,—no sorrow's reign,
No secret anguish, no corporeal pain;
No shivering limbs, no burning fever, there;
No soul's eclipse, no winter of despair.
    No night shall be in heaven.

Shrub Oak.

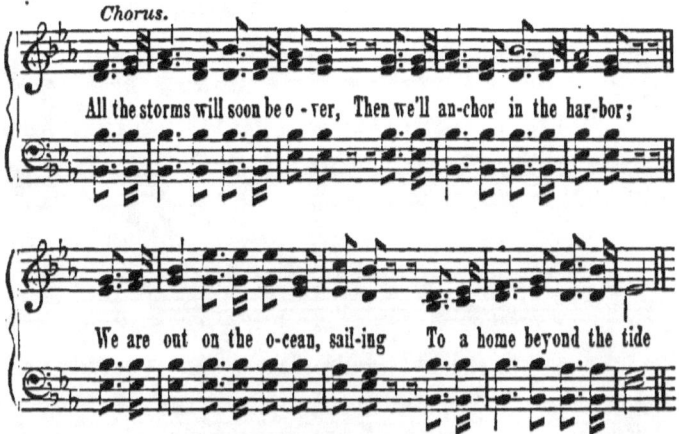

2 Millions now are safely landed
   Over on the golden shore;
   Millions more are on their journey,
   Yet there's room for millions more.
        All the storms, &c.

3 Come on board, and "ship" for glory,
   Be in haste—make up your mind!
   For our vessel's weighing anchor;
   You will soon be left behind.
        All the storms, &c.

4 You have kindred over yonder,
   On that bright and happy shore;
   By-and-by we'll swell the number,
   When the toils of life are o'er.
        All the storms, &c.

5 Spread your sails, while heavenly breezes
   Gently waft our vessel on;
   All on board are sweetly singing;
   Free salvation is the song.
        All the storms, &c.

6 When we all are safely anchor'd
   Over on the shining shore,
   We will walk about the city,
   And will sing for ever more.
        All the storms, &c.

Sibleyville.

Ca-naan's peaceful shore, Oh, sor-row shall come a-gain no more!

2 I seek not earthly glory, nor mingle with the gay;
  I covet not this world's gilded store:
 There are voices now calling from the bright realms of day,
  Oh, sorrow shall come again no more!
    'Tis a song, &c.

3 Though here I'm sad and drooping, and weep my life away,
  With a lone heart still clinging to the shore,
 Yet I hear happy voices which ever seem to say,
  Oh, sorrow shall come again no more!
    'Tis a song, &c.

4 'Tis a note that is wafted across the troubled wave;
  'Tis a song that I've heard upon the shore;
 'Tis a sweet-thrilling murmur around the Christian's grave:
  Oh, sorrow shall come again no more.
    'Tis a song, &c.

5 'Tis the loud-pealing anthem,—the victor's holy song,
  Where the strife and the conflict are o'er;
 Which the saved ones forever, in joyous notes, prolong,
  Oh, sorrow shall come again no more.
    'Tis a song, &c.

Spanish Hymn. 6s & 5s.

2 When shall love freely flow,
   Pure as life's river?
When shall sweet friendship glow
   Changeless forever?
Where joys celestial thrill,
Where bliss each heart shall fill,
And fears of parting chill,
   Never, no, never.

2 Oh, is it not written, "Believe and live"?
　　The heart, by bright hope allured,
　Shall find the comfort these words can give,
　　And be by its faith assured.
　Then why should we fear the cold world's frown,
　　When truth to the heart has given
　The light of religion to guide us on
　　In joy to the paths of heaven?

3 There is, there is, in thy holy word,
　　Thy word which can ne'er depart,
　There is a promise of mercy stored,
　　For the lowly and meek at heart.
　"My yoke is easy, my burden light;
　　Then come unto me for rest;"
　These, these are the words of promise stored
　　For the wounded and weary breast.

The Lord is my Shepherd.

1. The Lord is my shepherd; I | shall not | want.
2. He maketh me to lie down in green pastures; He leadeth me beside the still | wa- — | ters.
3. He restoreth my soul; he leadeth me In the paths of righteousness for his | name's— | sake.
4. Yea, though I walk through the valley of the shadow of death, I will fear no evil: for thou art with me; Thy rod and thy staff, they | *p* comfort | me.
5. Thou preparest a table before me in the presence of mine enemies, Thou anointest my head with oil;\/ my | cup .. runneth | over.
6. Surely goodness and mercy shall follow me all the days of my life; And I will dwell in the house of the Lord for- | ev- — | er. ‖ A-|men.

Father, I know.

1. Father, I know thy ways are just, Al- | though to me un-|known. ‖ Oh, grant me grace thy love to trust, And cry, | "Thy will be | done."
2. If thou shouldst hedge with thorns my path, Should | wealth and friends be- | gone, ‖ Still, with a firm and lively faith, I'll cry, | "Thy will be | done."
3. Although thy steps I cannot trace, Thy|sovereign right I'll | own ;‖ And, as instructed by thy grace, I'll cry, | "Thy will be | done."
4. 'Tis sweet thus passively to lie Be- | fore thy gracious | throne, ‖ Concerning every thing to cry, "My Father's | will be | done."

I will Arise.

1. I will arise, and go unto my Father, and will .. | say unto | him, ‖
2. Father, I have sinned against heav'n and be- | fore | thee, ‖
3. And am no more worthy to be called ... | thy | son. ‖ A -.. | men.

156

I will lift up mine eyes.

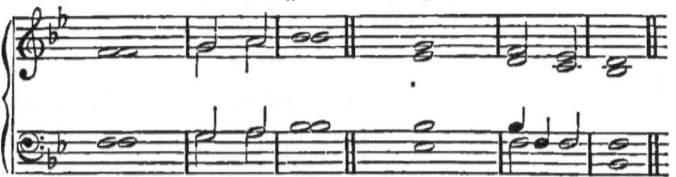

1. { I will lift up mine eyes unto the hills,
   From whence | cometh .. my | help.
2. { My help cometh from the Lord,
   Which made | heaven .. and | earth.
3. { He will not suffer thy foot to be moved.
   He that keepeth thee | will not | slumber.
4. { Behold, he that keepeth Israel
   Shall neither | slumber .. nor | sleep.
5. { The Lord is thy keeper;
   The sun is thy shade upon thy | right — | hand.
6. { The sun shall not smite thee by day,
   Nor the | *p* moon by | night.
7. { The Lord shall preserve thee from all evil:
   He shall pre- | serve thy | soul.
8. { The Lord shall preserve thy going out, and thy coming in,
   From this time forth, and even for evermore. | A- | men.

Gloria Patri.*

M. WALKER.

1. Glory be to the Father, and | to the | Son, ‖ and | to the | Holy|Ghost.
2. As it was in the beginning, | is | now, ‖ and ever | shall be, | world without end. A- | men. ‖

* This chant is adapted to the BENEDICTUS.

GENERAL INDEX.

Tunes marked thus (*) are Copyright; and are used in this work by permission of their proprietors.

	PAGE		PAGE		PAGE
Abba	116	Crosbie*	11	Illa*	18
Acushnet*	32	Dalston*	100	I'm a Pilgrim	143
Adelio*	70	Darley*	11	Indiana*	108
Agnes	32	Darwell*	91	Inverness	80
Ain	70	De Fleury	140	Iowa	81
America	102	Dedham	45	Italian Hymn	103
Amsterdam*	114	Dennis	77	Ives	109
Antioch*	32	Dove	141		
Anvern*	5	Dover	77	Jedburgh*	93
Ariel*	98	Downs*	45	Jordan*	52
Arietta	6	Duane Street*	12	Joy	104
Arlington	33	Duke Street*	13		
Arno	102	Dundee	46	Kenaz	143
Arnon	6			Kennet*	81
Ashley*	34	Easter Hymn	106		
Ashton*	135	Edenton*	98	Laban*	82
Athens*	35	Edinburgh	130	Land of Promise	144
Attila*	114	Effen*	13	Lanesboro'	52
Autumn*	117	Effingham	14	Laona	53
Ava*	103	Eglinton	78	Laurel*	53
Avon	35	Emmons	46	Lee	54
Aylesbury	72	Evan*	47	Lenox	94
Azmon*	36	Evening Hymn	14	Leroux	55
		Everest	53	Lisbon	82
Balaena	105			Lisher	94
Balerma	36	Federal Street*	15	Little*	55
Barby	37	Felton	141	Little Marlborough	83
Barre	72	Fletcher	47	Louvan*	18
Bartimeus	118	Folsom	136	Loving Kindness	19
Beethoven	7	Fountain	48	Lucas	145
Benevento	105	Frederick*	130	Lucius	56
Bertrand*	73			Lyons	136
Betah	118	Ganges	99		
Bethune*	91	Garland	48	Maclean	126
Beverly	73	Geneva	49	Marlow*	56
Blauveltville *	74	Gibson*	49	Martyn	110
Blendon	9	Gleason*	15	Martyrdom	35
Boylston	74	Golan	16	Massillon*	56
Bradford	37	Golden Hill	78	Mazzaroth*	83
Brattle Street	38	Gorton	78	Meade*	72
Breck*	38	Goshen	131	Mear	57
Brightness*	134	Gratitude	6	Mede	57
Browne	75	Greenville	120	Medfield	58
Brownell *	8	Guardian	132	Mendon*	20
Bruce	128			Meriden*	59
Burlington*	139	Haddam	92	Metropolis	58
		Hamburg	16	Migdol*	21
Cambridge	33	Happy Day	17	Missionary Chant*	20
Canaan	40	Happy Voices	141	Missionary Hymn*	115
Canopus	134	Harmonia*	92	Moravian	60
Captivity*	9	Harwell*	120	Mornington	84
Cazenovia	41	Haverhill*	79	Mount Pisgah	60
Charity Hymn	76	Heber	50		
Chester	119	Hebron	17	Narenza	87
China	42	Hendon	107	Nashville*	100
Christian Victory	129	Henry	50	Nettleton*	121
Christmas	42	Hereford	79	Newbury	93
Clapton*	76	Herrick	80	No Night in Heaven*	146
Clarendon	43	Hesville*	107	Nuremburg	110
Come to Jesus	130	Hinton	131		
Come, ye Disconsolate	135	Home	132	Oatlands	61
Come, ye Sinners	119	Homeward Bound*	142	Old Hundred	22
Corelli	76	Horton	108	Olga*	147
Coronation*	44	Howard	51	Oliphant*	126
Coventry	44			Olivet*	104
Creation	10	I do Believe	51	Olmutz	84

METRICAL INDEX.

	PAGE		PAGE		PAGE
Olney	85	Seir*	86	Triumph	96
Omicron*	22	Selma	87		
Ortonville*	62	Shining Shore*	148	Unity	152
Otto*	121	Shirland	87	Uxbridge	28
		Shrub Oak* (A Home		Varina	67
Park Street	23	beyond the tide)	148	Villenova	28
Peekskill*	23	Sibleyville* (Sorrow		Violet	153
Pentonville	85	come again no more)	150		
Peoria, or Eden	137	Sicilian Hymn	122	Ward*	28
Peters	101	Sidmouth	113	Ware*	29
Piety*	62	Siloam*	63	Warsaw	96
Pleyel's Hymn	110	Silver Street	88	Warwick	68
Plymouth	86	Smyrna	123	Washington Square	53
Pomeroy	147	Southwell	88	Watchman	90
Portuguese Hymn	133	Spanish Hymn	151	Webb*	116
Power	114	St. Ann's	64	Wells	29
		State Street	89	Welton	30
Reliance*	24	Stephens	64	Weymouth	97
Remember Me	63	Sterling	26	Whitefield	68
Rest*	24	St. John's	64	Williams	30
Rockingham*	25	St. Louis	27	Will you Go	153
Rock of Ages*	111	St. Martin's	65	Wilmot	125
Rosefield*	111	Stockwell*	124	Windham	31
Roslyn	112	Stonefield	27	Wings of a Dove	154
Rothwell	25	St. Thomas	89	Woodstock	69
Royalton	112	Swanwick	66		
		Switzer	124	Zalah	154
Savannah	129			Zarephath*	31
Saxony	122	Tappan*	66	Zerah*	69
Scotland	138	Thatcher	90	Zion*	127
Seasons	26	Thornton	125		

METRICAL INDEX.

L. M.

Anvern	5
Arietta	6
Arnon	6
Beethoven	7
Blendon	9
Brownell	8
Captivity	9
Creation	10
Crosbie	11
Darley	11
Duane Street	12
Duke Street	13
Effen	13
Effingham	14
Evening Hymn	14
Federal Street	15
Gleason	15
Golan	16
Gratitude	6
Hamburg	16
Happy Day	17
Hebron	17
Illa	18
Louvan	18
Loving Kindness	19
Mendon	20
Migdol	21
Missionary Chant	20
Old Hundred	22
Omicron	22
Park Street	23
Peekskill	23
Reliance	24
Rest	24
Rockingham	25
Rothwell	25
Seasons	26
Sterling	26
St. Louis	27
Stonefield	27
Uxbridge	28
Villenova	28
Ward	28
Ware	29
Wells	29
Welton	30
Williams	30
Windham	31
Zarephath	31

C. M.

Acushnet	32
Agnes	32
Antioch	32
Arlington	33
Ashley	34
Athens	35
Avon	35
Azmon	36
Balerma	36
Barby	37
Bradford	37
Brattle Street	38
Breck	38
Cambridge	39
Canaan	40
Cazenovia	41
China	42
Christmas	42
Clarendon	43
Coronation	44
Coventry	44
Dedham	45
Downs	45
Dundee	46
Emmons	46
Evan	47
Everest	53
Fletcher	47
Fountain	48
Garland	48
Geneva	49
Gibson	49
Heber	50
Henry	50
Howard	51
I do Believe	51
Jordan	52
Lanesboro'	52
Laona	53
Laurel	53
Lee	54
Leroux	55
Little	55
Lucius	56
Marlow	56
Martyrdom	35

METRICAL INDEX.

	PAGE
Massillon	56
Mear	57
Mede	57
Medfield	58
Metropolis	58
Meriden	59
Moravian	60
Mount Pisgah	60
Oatlands	61
Ortonville	62
Piety	62
Remember Me	63
Siloam	63
St. Ann's	64
Stephens	64
St. John's	64
St. Martin's	65
Swanwick	66
Tappan	66
Varina	67
Warwick	68
Washington Square	53
Whitefield	68
Woodstock	69
Zerah	69

S. M.

	PAGE
Adello	70
Ain	70
Aylesbury	72
Barre	72
Bertrand	73
Beverly	73
Blauveltville	74
Boylston	74
Browne	75
Charity Hymn	76
Clapton	76
Corelli	76
Dennis	77
Dover	77
Eglinton	78
Golden Hill	78
Gorton	78
Haverhill	79
Hereford	79
Herrick	80
Inverness	80
Iowa	81
Kennet	81
Laban	82
Lisbon	82
Little Marlborough	83
Mazzaroth	83
Meade	72
Mornington	84
Narenza	87
Olmutz	84
Olney	85
Pentonville	85
Plymouth	86
Seir	86
Selma	87
Shirland	87
Silver Street	88
Southwell	89
State Street	89
St. Thomas	89
Thatcher	90
Watchman	90

H. M.

	PAGE
Bethune	91

	PAGE
Darwell	91
Haddam	92
Harmonia	92
Jedburgh	93
Lenox	94
Lisher	94
Newbury	95
Triumph	96
Warsaw	96
Weymouth	97

C. P. M.

	PAGE
Ariel	98
Edenton	98
Ganges	99

L. P. M.

	PAGE
Nashville	100

S. P. M.

	PAGE
Dalston	100
Peters	101

6s, 4s.

	PAGE
America	102
Arno	102
Ava	103
Italian Hymn	103
Olivet	104

6s, 9s.

	PAGE
Joy	104

7s.

	PAGE
Balaena	105
Benevento	105
Easter Hymn	106
Hendon	107
Hessville	107
Horton	108
Indiana	108
Ives	109
Martyn	110
Nuremburg	110
Pleyel's Hymn	110
Rock of Ages	111
Rosefield	111
Roslyn	112
Royalton	112
Sidmouth	113

7s, 6s.

	PAGE
Amsterdam	114
Ashton	155
Attila	114
Missionary Hymn	115
Power	114
Webb	116

8s, 7s.

	PAGE
Abba	116
Autumn	117
Bartimeus	118
Retah	118
Chester	119
Come, ye Sinners	119
Greenville	120
Harwell	120
Nettleton	121
Otto	121
Saxony	122
Sicilian Hymn	122
Smyrna	123
Stockwell	124

	PAGE
Switzer	124
Thornton	125
Violet	153
Wilmot	125

8s, 7s, & 4s.

	PAGE
Maclean	126
Oliphant	126
Zion	127

8s, 7s, & 5s.

	PAGE
Bruce	128

10s.

	PAGE
Christian Victory	129
Savannah	129

11s.

	PAGE
Edinburgh	130
Frederick	130
Goshen	131
Guardian	132
Hinton	131
Home	132
Portuguese Hymn	133

11s, 10s.

	PAGE
Brightness	134
Come, ye Disconsolate	135
Folsom	136
Lyons	136

12s.

	PAGE
Scotland	138

12s, 11s.

	PAGE
Peoria, or Eden	137

12s, 11s, & 8s.

	PAGE
Burlington	139

PECULIAR.

	PAGE
Canopus (Ere I sleep)	134
Come to Jesus	139
De Fleury	140
Dove	141
Felton	141
Happy Voices	141
Homeward Bound	142
I'm a Pilgrim	143
Kenaz	143
Land of Promise	144
Lucas	145
No Night in Heaven	146
Olga	147
Pomeroy	147
Shining Shore	148
Shrub Oak (A Home beyond the tide)	148
Sibleyville (Sorrow come again no more)	150
Spanish Hymn	151
Unity	152
Will you Go	153
Wings of a Dove	154
Zalah	155

CHANTS.

	PAGE
Father I Know	156
Gloria Patrie	157
I will Arise	156
I will lift up mine Eyes	157
The Lord is my Shepherd	156

www.ingramcontent.com/pod-product-compliance
Lightning Source LLC
Chambersburg PA
CBHW030306170426
43202CB00009B/889